CW00591752

SHELVE IT

Dek Messecar
Series Consultant Editor: Bob Tattersall

CONTENTS

COLLINS

Introduction

A shelf is any horizontal surface that can be used to store or display an object. This deceptively simple statement ignores the hundreds of ways that have been developed for making and supporting shelves.

Although there seems to be an infinite variety of shelves, for the purpose of this book they are divided into three categories: wall-mounted shelves, built-in shelves and free-standing shelves. Any of these can be single shelves or 'shelf units' (shelves that are assembled with sides or struts, making a box shape).

If you are thinking of buying or making shelves, there are (apart from price) only three considerations. The shelves must be a size and strength that will support the load placed on them. They must be of a type of construction that can be used in your chosen situation. Lastly, the overall design must

Right. *Deep, built-in shelves fill an alcove and adjustable shelving allows objects of a similar size to be grouped together.*

Centre right, below. *A high-tech shelf system designed for use in warehouses. Combined with plain wooden shelves, this makes a stylish bookshelf.*

Far right, below. *Built-in wooden shelving. Simple to construct and very useful in family rooms.*

Centre right, above. *Track shelving used to advantage in a tiny office. The shelves have been "wrapped" in plastic, as has the work-surface.*

Far right, above. *The supports for these dark green shelves have been painted white and are made of architrave off-cuts. The shelves are removable for easy window cleaning.*

create an effect that pleases you and is sympathetic to the style of the rest of the room.

This book shows you how to choose suitable shelves for different purposes and places, and helps you decide whether to make them yourself or buy them. The photographs will give you an idea of some of the effects that are possible, and perhaps spark off an idea that will solve a storage problem or finish a difficult corner or alcove.

Plan your project thoroughly, no matter how simple it seems. Always make a sketch of your design (to see that it will actually fit together) and show details of fixings. Then, try to imagine the various stages of assembly. This can save a lot of redesign during building when you may find yourself going about it the hard way.

WALL-MOUNTED SHELVES

Fixing shelves to one wall (as opposed to spanning between two) is one of the easiest and most versatile methods. The only requirement is a reasonably flat wall that is sound enough to take the load. With all the variations on this theme, the strength of the brackets, track systems, cantilever fixtures etc., is usually far greater than you're ever likely to need. The weak link is nearly always the wall fixing. However, any wall of brick or building block is quite strong enough for most purposes, and partition (hollow) walls are fine, provided the fixings are screwed to the vertical timbers inside them.

The most basic support is the **simple bracket** that is fixed below the shelf. Traditional ones were made of wood, brass, cast iron, or wrought iron scrollwork, and there are many beautiful examples for sale in antique shops. In fact, these have become so popular that reproductions are being manufactured. Modern designs, made of pressed steel, are the cheapest ready-made shelf support available.

A popular extension of the bracket idea is the **track system.** This consists of vertical metal (or, less often, wood) strips fixed to the wall. Adjustable brackets are attached to the strips by means of holes, slots, or some can slide to any position and be locked in place.

Further refinements that attach to the vertical tracks include light fittings with concealed wiring, bookends, partitions, and cabinet brackets to allow cupboards, desks and drawer units to be mounted as well as shelves. You can also use these systems to completely fit out the interior of cupboards and wardrobes, as there are clothes rail fittings, too.

Some manufacturers make only tracks and brackets, while others offer shelves, and furniture, too. As the different brands are not interchangeable, it's a good idea to collect as many catalogues as possible before buying. You may want to extend your system later on.

Above left. *Simple black brackets with veneered blockboard shelves provide storage space in a kitchen too small for cupboards.*

Left. *These commercially produced shelves are cheap and easy to fix.*

Above. *A single shelf running round the kitchen above the work surface. Fixed with cantilever brackets and tiled to match.*

Left. *Keep a look out for lovely old shelf brackets like this one. They can often be found in second-hand shops. Modern reproductions are also available, but will cost a lot more.*

Shelf support brackets, whether single or mounted on tracks, are the easiest solution to DIY shelves. By buying ready-finished shelves in standard sizes, or having them cut to length by the supplier, you can put up a roomful of shelves in a day with no woodworking at all.

Cantilever fittings make it possible to fit shelves without any visible means of support. They are metal rods that are set into walls and into holes in the back edge of the shelf.

Shelf units (i.e. more than one shelf attached to uprights) and cupboards can be mounted directly to walls by fixing small metal angle brackets or a wood batten at the bottom to support the weight. Then the top of the unit is fastened to the wall to prevent it leaning outward. Small, unobtrusive metal plates are usually sufficient for this.

Finally, there are some shelves that are designed to be hung on wires or ropes attached to the wall or ceiling.

Right. *Glass shelves on tracks, fitted in front of this bathroom window, make a perfect place for plants. The edge of the glass shelves should be ground.*

Top left. *A simple opening bridged by glass shelves and a collection of bottles is an attractive feature in this room. In this instance the shelves are not fixed to allow for easy cleaning, but this would not always be safe.*

Top right. *Unusual wall-mounted fittings support generous-sized kitchen shelving. The supports must be securely attached to a very solid wall as they may be expected to carry heavy items such as crockery.*

Left. *A system that completely covers two walls of this room and provides different width shelves for various purposes. A perfect solution for a small family room or bedsittingroom.*

Fixing wall-mounted shelves

The first concern when fixing shelves to walls is the type and condition of the wall. Strong fixings in masonry walls are easily made with screws and plugs or, for unusually heavy loads, expansion bolts. The main thing to remember is that plaster isn't strong, and so all holes must be drilled deep enough so that the plugs can be pushed through the plaster and into the wall itself.

Hollow partition walls can be awkward, as strong fixings can only be made to the vertical timbers (studs) inside them. The studs are usually not more than 600mm apart, equally spaced in the wall, but may not be in the places you want the brackets or tracks. You should be able to find the studs by knocking on the wall, moving from side to side. The spaces between studs should sound hollow and the studs, solid. This method works easily with modern plasterboard, but some old lathe and plaster walls can disguise the sound very effectively.

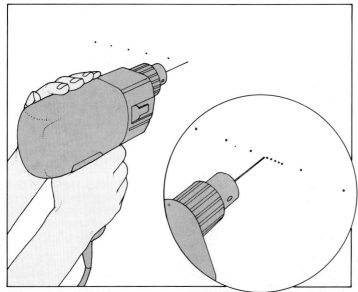

Using Shelf Brackets

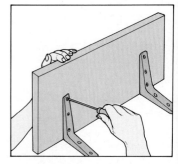

For small shelves, it's easiest to screw the brackets to the shelf and then hold it up to the wall.

Use a spirit level on the shelf or have someone stand back and tell you when it's straight. Then mark the positions of the screw holes with a pencil or bradawl.

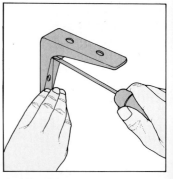

For long shelves, or where the brackets must be located on studs, it's easier to put the brackets on the wall first.

In this case, you will have to find the studs by drilling tiny holes about 25mm apart until you come to solid wood. Do this along the line of the proposed shelf, so you won't need to fill and redecorate the wall.

Find the edges of the stud by drilling more holes close together and marking the first hole either side that just misses it. Repeat the process about 600mm to one side of the first one, and then measure the distance from the centre of one stud to the next. Hopefully, the other studs will be the same distance apart.

Fix one bracket at the correct height and then hold another against the wall, with the shelf resting on both.

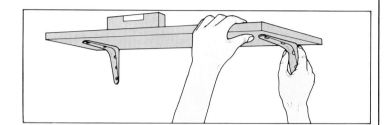

If the shelf sags, hold it on its edge to set the level of the second bracket. Once the two end brackets are fixed, find the height of any middle brackets the same way. This ensures the shelf will be straight.

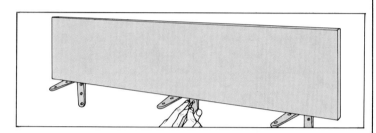

Lay the first shelf on the brackets and measure for any shelves above or below. Put up all the remaining brackets before fixing the shelves to them.

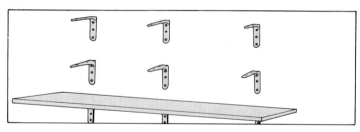

Place the top shelf in position and hang a plumb line (or a string with a weight) over the side. Line up each subsequent shelf with the string and fix to the brackets.

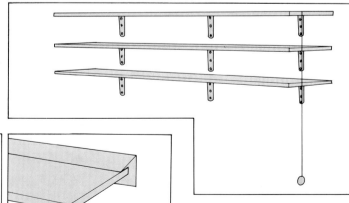

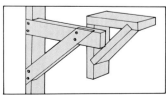

You can make your own wooden brackets and use plugs to hide the screw heads.

Here's a novel bracket made to take standard chipboard shelving. The shelf is inserted,

covering the wall fixings, and it will support quite a heavy load without sagging.

Putting up Track Systems

Track systems are fixed in much the same way as single brackets. If necessary, cut the uprights to length with a hacksaw, but be sure to have the uncut ends at the top when putting them up.

Decide the height of one of the tracks and mark the position of the top fixing hole. If you wish (or if your tracks are infinitely adjustable, i.e. without holes or slots for the brackets), you can use a spirit level and straight batten (or a shelf on edge) to draw a horizontal line on the wall at the height of the first hole. However, it's safer to put up the first track and then use a shelf to set the height of the other end, so you can see how it looks.

Exactly level might not look quite right. If a doorway, wall or ceiling is out of true, you'll find it's the shelves that appear wrong.

Drill and plug the top hole in the usual way. Screw the track to the wall without tightening, so the track is free to swing to a vertical position. Mark all the remaining fixing holes.

Swing the track to one side to drill and plug the other holes, and then screw it tightly to the wall.

To find the height of the next track, fit a bracket to the corresponding holes or slots in two tracks and place a shelf on edge over the brackets. Then use a spirit level or let a helper tell you when it looks horizontal. If you have trouble deciding, put up more brackets and loose shelves until it's right.

When the tracks and brackets are up, fix the shelves in position using a plumb line, as for single brackets.

If you want the back edges of the shelves to touch the wall, you can cut notches in the back edge around the tracks.

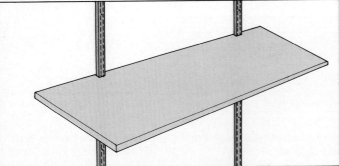

Fixing shelf units to walls

Small shelf units, such as spice racks and what-nots can be fixed with small brass mirror plates arranged to be as unobtrusive as possible.

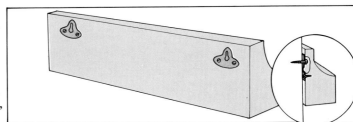

Larger units such as bookshelves, corner cupboards, etc., need support at the bottom, as well.

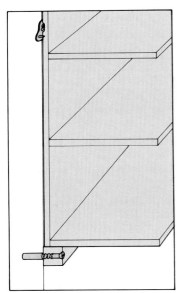

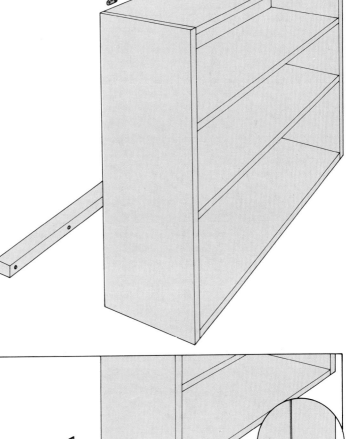

The strongest support is a batten, screwed to the wall underneath. Pins, driven through the bottom into the batten, will prevent it slipping off, and the plates at the top stop it leaning away from the wall.

A less visible method, although not quite as strong, is to fix thin brackets to the wall. The important thing is that the shelf must rest right in the corner of the bracket – any gap will allow the bracket to bend under load.

By using several brackets, any but the heaviest loads can be supported.

BUILT-IN SHELVES

Visually, built-in shelves offer attractive, simple lines that blend with the room and become part of it. The practical advantage is that all the available space is used and the awkward places between walls and shelf units and dust traps are kept to a minimum.

While there are many examples of ready-made 'built-in' kitchen units and bedroom cupboards on the market, shelves don't lend themselves so readily to mass-produced designs that can be truly described as built-in. There are free-standing shelf units that are made in several widths and are meant to be combined to fill various heights and widths of wall space. However, built-in shelves mean some work shaping them to fit the space.

From a construction point of view, 'built-in' means using the walls as a part of the structure. While this is the best method to use in some cases, quite often it is easier to make a complete structure without using the walls, place it in position, and then disguise the joins between shelf unit and walls to make it look built-in. The advantage of this approach is that the shelves and uprights can be made straight and square instead of having to be shaped to the walls, floor and ceiling. Also, if only two or three shelves are permanently fixed to the uprights, the other shelves can rest on adjustable supports.

Another approach for the built-in look is to build the necessary upright supports to look like walls, rather than thin panels like the shelves, effectively adding walls that the shelves can be built-in to.

A work surface can be thought of as a large shelf, and can be used as a desk, table or kitchen counter top. Once in place, it can be the basis for smaller shelves, above and below.

Above. *Alcoves fitted with built-in shelving from floor to ceiling provide perfect storage for a large collection of books and small mementoes.*

Right. *The uprights for these shelves have been made of plasterboard and decorated to be part of the structure of the room. Shelves have been fixed at a* variety of heights to allow for display of different sized books and objects.

Above left. *A very simple way to fit shelves in an alcove. Painting them the same colour as the walls has made them much more interesting.*

Above right. *This alcove was formed when cupboards were being fitted. The interior has been decorated and independently lit to provide display for a collection of wooden toys.*

Right. *Close-up of the strips which can be used to give variation in height of the individual shelves, enabling you to tailor the system for your specific needs.*

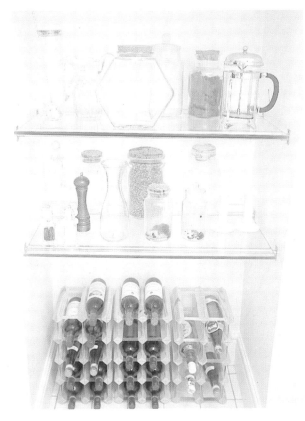

Top right. *These painted wooden shelves have a back to keep them rigid and form useful storage for a child of any age.*

Above left. *The uprights in these shelves have been drilled at regular intervals so that the owner has complete adjustability. The shelves are glass, but the method works very well with other types of shelf.*

Left. *The simple brass rod and fittings which hold these shelves can be bought in any hardware shop. They are available in brass and chrome and in a variety of sizes. Experiment with the placing of the rod to gain as much support and the best visual effect. It would not be advisable to span too large an alcove in this way.*

Fixing built-in shelves

The least expensive method of making shelves is to rest them on wood battens that are fixed to the walls of an alcove. Alcoves seem to offer an almost ready-made site for shelves. After all, there is a wall at the back and at each side to hold the supports. However, this method is not quite as simple as it looks: if the walls aren't straight or square with each other, each shelf must be shaped to fit the space it will occupy. Also, if the walls are very uneven, the supports won't fit flat against them. However, if the shelves are for books or will be well-filled, there will be very little of the shelves showing.

So, if the side walls are fairly flat and you don't mind the shelves not quite touching the back wall, it is only necessary to make the front edges of the shelves even with each other and the corner of the chimney breast. Otherwise, you can scribe each shelf into the alcove as described in the Tools and Techniques section.

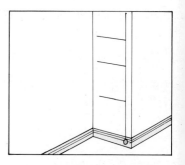

Mark the wall for the position of the front edge of each shelf by using a plumb line.

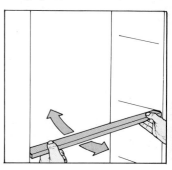

Then cut a piece of batten to length and get a helper to hold it across the alcove as if it were the front edge of a shelf (or you can use a small piece of wood to wedge it into place). Stand back and look at it from different angles, adjusting the batten until it looks straight. Mark the other wall, and use a plumb line on that side to mark the position of the shelf fronts.

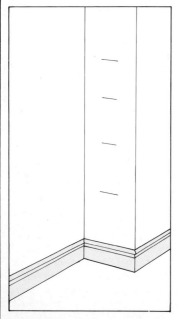

Measure the height of the alcove from the top of the skirting board and mark the approximate position of the shelves. It is usual for the spaces between the shelves to be larger at the bottom and reduce towards the top, but decide according to what you intend putting on the shelves.

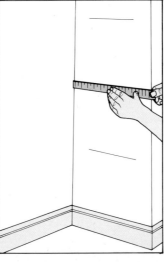

The front edges of the shelves should be slightly recessed into the alcove, and in line with each other. Measure the depth of the alcove at each mark, and make sure your shelves will fit into the narrowest part without sticking out. If necessary, you can cut all the shelves to the depth of the narrowest one; or, if this would mean some of them being too far from the back wall, use wider shelves and scribe the back of the protruding ones.

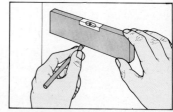

Mark the position of one of the shelves on one wall, using a spirit level to make sure the line is horizontal.

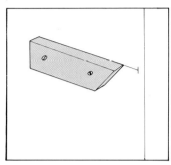

Cut a batten support to length and fix it so the top edge aligns with the mark. To be unobtrusive, the batten supports should be slightly recessed behind the front edge of the shelf, and the appearance will be further improved if you chamfer or round the front of the batten.

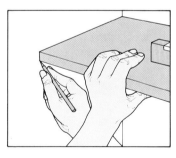

Cut a shelf to length and hold one end on the fixed support with a level resting on the top. Adjust the free end up and down until it is level, and draw a line on the wall along the bottom of the shelf, also marking the position of the front edge.

Then measure the length of the batten support for that side and fix it to the wall with the top edge aligned with the pencil mark. Place the shelf in position and check whether it is sitting properly on both supports.

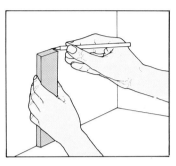

Now cut a piece of batten (or use a measuring tape) to set the height of the next shelf. Mark the wall at the top of the batten at each corner, and fix the next support in position. Then cut and hold the next shelf in position and proceed as with the first shelf.

To prevent shelves sagging
An easy and effective way to keep thin shelves from sagging under heavy loads, is to fix a batten to the wall along the back edge. Cut these to fit and fix them flush with the top edge of the side battens.

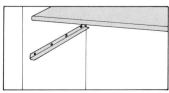

Instead of using battens, another method is to screw lengths of

thin metal angle (instead of battens) to the walls. The shelves can set on the flanges and be fixed from underneath. Be sure to make the shelves a loose fit so there's room for the thickness of the angle between the edge of the shelf and the wall.

Alcove shelf supports
Here's an alternative method for alcove supports. It looks best with glass shelves, but it would work with wood or man-made boards.

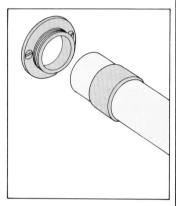

Buy wardrobe hanging rail (tube) and enough socket end fittings to make two supports for each shelf. These are available from DIY shops in chrome or brass finish and several sizes – 18mm or 25mm diameter is about right.

Measure the positions of the shelves as described above, and screw one end fitting to the wall. The tubes should be placed about $\frac{1}{4}$ of the shelf width from the edges. Then cut the tube to a length that allows you to insert one end into the fitting with the other fitting in place. Be careful that, once in position, the tube cannot slide far enough to come out of either socket.

Built-in units

Sometimes an easier method is to make a shelf unit with two sides and all shelves the same size. This should be made small enough to fit into the alcove at the narrowest and shallowest point. This reduces the amount of scribing to shape you have to do. It's only necessary to screw the bottom, middle and top shelves to the uprights; the others can rest on bookcase strips or adjustable shelf supports.

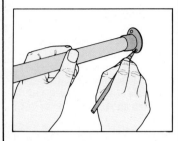

Hold it in position to mark the holes for the other end. Drill and plug the holes and then screw the second fitting to the wall with the tube in place.

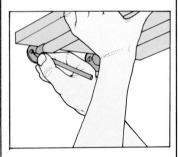

Repeat for the second tube, but place the shelf in position to mark the final holes. This will ensure the shelf rests along the full length of both tubes.

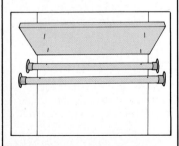

If the shelves are wood or man-made board, you can prevent then slipping off the tubes by driving 4 small nails into the bottom of the shelf and clipping the heads off. These can sit in holes drilled in the tubes.

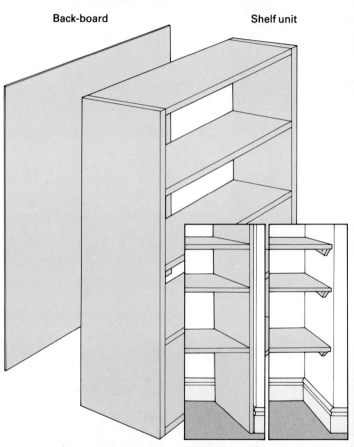

Back-board   Shelf unit

If the shelves don't fit against the back wall very well, you can put a panel of thin plywood, chipboard (particle board), or hardboard onto the back of the unit. You can, of course, decorate the face of the back panel before fixing it to the shelves, and still have the effect of seeing the wall between the shelves.

Corners
If you are building shelves into a corner, you again have to choose between using batten supports on the wall or making a second upright. In this case, the two-sided shelf unit is more desirable, as it will be difficult to make the shelves meet the wall as perfectly as they will fit the upright.

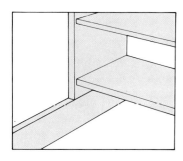

One way to deal with the skirting board, is to let the upright sit on top of it, but this may look awkward. It also makes the addition of a trim to the front of the upright difficult.

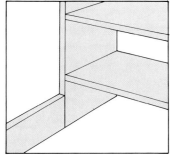

Another way is to cut the required length of skirting board away with a tenon saw. If the wall isn't straight and vertical (and what wall is?) then there may still be a difficult front edge to trim.

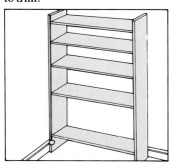

The best solution is to place the unit in position as close as

possible to the wall and use a plumb line or level to make sure the uprights are vertical.

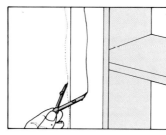

Then, any gap, however awkward, can be bridged by scribing a trimming piece to the wall.

Additional support
If the shelves are not going to be adjustable, you can put partitions in between them. These can be placed at random, or arranged to accommodate particular items, such as hi-fi, etc. If you place them in line with each other, use wire shelf supports to hold them in place.

This method makes a very strong unit, as the load on each shelf is shared with all those below.

A plinth under the bottom shelf, or feet beneath the bottom partitions, will allow you to make thin, long shelves to carry very heavy loads.

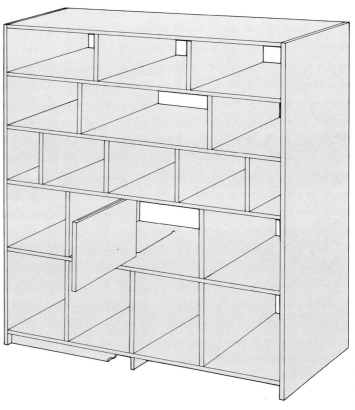

FREE-STANDING SHELVES

Free-standing shelves are any that you would consider as separate pieces of furniture – shelves that you could move from one room or house to the next, even though there may be some fixings to the walls or ceiling.

Apart from making them yourself, there are hundreds of manufactured pieces and systems. In general, this type of shelving is more expensive than the DIY types (some are very expensive). However, pieces of furniture that you can keep for years are a sort of investment. This is true of good quality systems that can be added to gradually, as you can afford them. Also, some systems cost very little more than DIY shelves, and the amount of work required to assemble a ready-made, free-standing set of shelves is considerably less.

One of the most popular systems consists of *upright metal or wood ladders* that carry shelves (as well as desks, cupboards and drawer units) between them.

Cubes that stack up are a versatile system. Most of these incorporate a means of fixing the cubes together and they can sometimes be wall-mounted. Also you can mix DIY shelves with them to make desks and extra shelves.

Poles or posts of wood or metal are made with adjustable feet at both ends. They are placed vertically between the floor and ceiling and the feet are screwed out until the post is effectively held by the pressure. Four of these then carry adjustable shelves between them. Pairs of posts can be added to extend the system sideways.

There are systems of *tubes* or *struts* that are held together with corner fittings. These build into frames that support shelves, and there are systems of flat panels that clip together into cubes. These offer some possibility for varying the overall size. You can have the glass cut to your size, but be sure to ask for the edges to be ground and polished.

Top far left. *Designed for shop-window display, a unit like this can easily be used in a home setting.*

Bottom far left. *Used as a room divider, this unit is given added permenency by the addition of a wooden strip where it meets the ceiling.*

Above left. *Another free-standing unit used as a room divider. This one is slightly raised off the floor and attached to the wall on either side.*

Left. *A cube system, of which there are a number available, can be built into whatever shape you want without any DIY skills. A variation in the components purchased gives each arrangement individuality.*

Above. *This system relies upon the four uprights being adjusted between the floor and ceiling correctly before the shelves are added. Follow the instructions carefully.*

Designing a free-standing unit

Designing and making your own free-standing shelf units is not very different from built-in ones, apart from the lateral support needed to prevent them from leaning side to side. A quick look at the ready-made systems will show you the various devices that can provide this support. Otherwise, you can use the same sort of support as for a built-in or wall-mounted unit. Any ceiling or wall fixing (such as mirror plates) will prevent the top of the unit moving sideways in relation to the bottom.

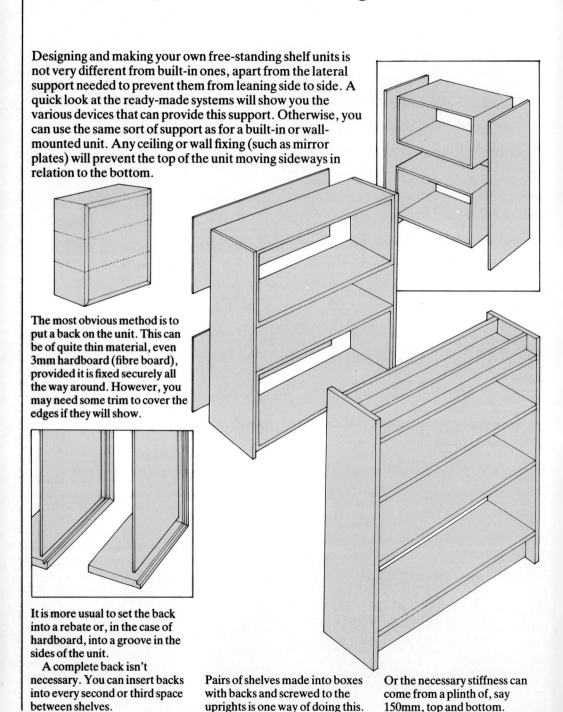

The most obvious method is to put a back on the unit. This can be of quite thin material, even 3mm hardboard (fibre board), provided it is fixed securely all the way around. However, you may need some trim to cover the edges if they will show.

It is more usual to set the back into a rebate or, in the case of hardboard, into a groove in the sides of the unit.

A complete back isn't necessary. You can insert backs into every second or third space between shelves.

Pairs of shelves made into boxes with backs and screwed to the uprights is one way of doing this.

Or the necessary stiffness can come from a plinth of, say 150mm, top and bottom.

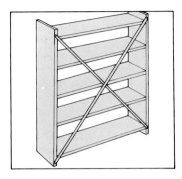

Diagonal braces are an often used method. These can be wooden struts, wire, metal rod or wood dowel.

No matter which of these methods you choose, remember that the stability depends on the overall height in relation to the length and width of the bottom. A tall, shallow bookshelf, no matter how rigid, will not stand alone safely.

One way around this, without fixing to the ceiling or wall, is to add a unit at right angles to the first.

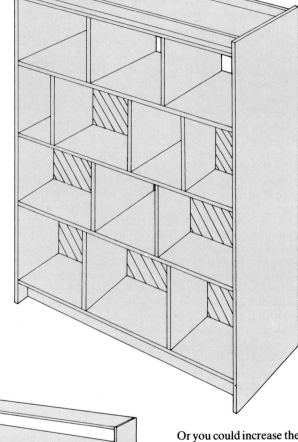

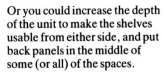

Or you could increase the depth of the unit to make the shelves usable from either side, and put back panels in the middle of some (or all) of the spaces.

23

Materials

The most widely used materials for shelves are solid wood, chipboard (particle board), blockboard, plywood and medium density fibreboard (MDF). These are all readily available and some can be bought partly or fully finished as shelves. If you want to do all the cutting to size yourself, timber merchants and large DIY chainstores are the cheapest place to buy them. However, many smaller DIY stores offer a cut to size service, and the effort saved is well worth the difference in price. Before placing your order, be sure to ask whether the cuts will be clean, straight and square; unfortunately, some cutting services are meant only to make pieces small enough to fit into your car.

Wood is the traditional material but, although it's the stiffest and strongest, it does have some drawbacks. It is expensive in comparison with the others, and is difficult to obtain in widths greater than about 250mm. Since wide pieces tend to warp or split more than narrow ones, it's usual to join narrower pieces edge to edge. A sufficiently strong joint can be made with ordinary woodworking glue and clamping until set, but the edges must be perfectly straight to make a close fit.

The growth rings in the wood should face opposite directions to minimize warping.

If you want wood shelves for a wall-mounted track system or brackets, you can use narrow widths as slats.

It's also worthwhile looking at ready-made wood shelves, available in standard lengths. Some are fully finished and others ready to finish as you choose.

If you're making a shelf unit or built-in shelves, the structure will help to hold the wood straight.

Chipboard (particle board) is the most popular material for shelves, probably because it is the least expensive, and comes in shelf size widths (as well as large sheets) with many different coverings.

Because of its lack of stiffness, chipboard needs support at closer intervals than other shelf materials.

The finishes available are real wood veneers, decorative PVC coatings, and melamine (usually limited to white, cream and imitation woodgrain) which is a very hardwearing, easy to clean surface.

You can buy chipboard in different widths with all the surface covered except the ends. After cutting to length, these are finished with matching iron-on strip.

Blockboard is made of a core of softwood battens held together by one or two layers of veneer on each face. Used with the core in the direction of the shelf's length, it is stiffer than chipboard. But as it is sold mainly in sheets, all the edges need finishing and there are sometimes gaps between the battens that can be awkward when fixing into the edges.

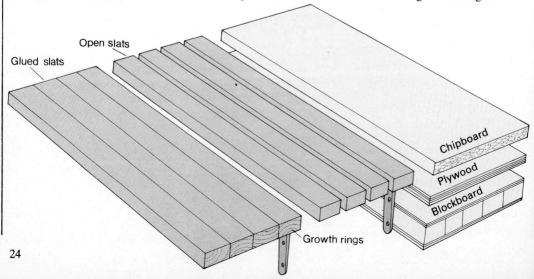

Glued slats

Open slats

Chipboard

Plywood

Blockboard

Growth rings

Different facings include many wood veneers and also plastic laminates.

Plywood is strong and more uniform than blockboard, but not quite as stiff. Again, it is sold in sheets rather than shelf widths and comes plain or with veneer or plastic laminate faces.

Medium density fibreboard (MDF) is sold in sheets and is probably the best material if you're going to paint the shelves. It has a very smooth surface that is without grain and is comparable to chipboard in strength and stiffness, although a little heavier. It is inexpensive, cuts very cleanly, can be shaped in any direction and doesn't have to be covered on the edges.

Hardboard is not exactly a shelving material, but it's used for backs of shelf units and cabinets. It is actually high density fibreboard and the most used thicknesses are 3mm and (less often) 6mm. It usually has one smooth face and one rough. The smooth side is suitable for

painting, but you can also buy hardboard with a white enamel or melamine surface that matches white melamine covered chipboard. Used together, it is possible to make a shelf unit that requires no finishing at all.

Glass can be bought in sheets, but it makes sense to buy it cut to size from a glazier or DIY store.

Glass shelves need to have their edges ground smooth and polished, and your supplier will be able to advise on the best thickness and type of glass to use. This will depend on the size of the shelves, the method used to support them and what you intend to put on them. Plate glass 6mm thick is suitable for shelves up to 1m long which will carry light loads.

SUPPORTS

As well as strength, shelves must have enough stiffness not to sag under load. All materials (except glass) will bend a great deal before there's any chance of breaking. Remember that the shelf is likely to be supporting the load for a long time.

As a rough guide, these distances between supports would be suitable for bookshelves. As books (and records) are probably the heaviest item, lighter loads won't need so many. If you're using brackets, you can always add extra ones if you find the shelves tend to sag. For shelf units and built-in shelves, it's better to have too much support, rather than too little. Also, you can double the distances between supports by fixing wood battens either to the shelves to stiffen them, or on the wall behind.

Material	Distance Between Supports
12mm chipboard	300mm
15mm chipboard	400mm
18mm chipboard 15mm chipboard 18mm MDF	500mm
18mm plywood 18mm blockboard 25mm MDF 18mm wood (finished about 15mm)	700mm
25mm wood (finished about 21mm)	900mm

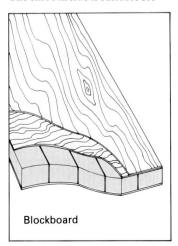

Blockboard

Fittings

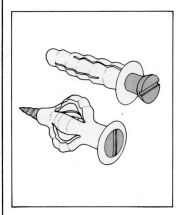

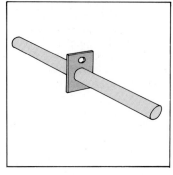

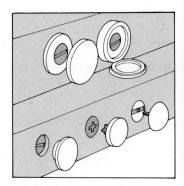

Fixing to brick, stone or building block walls is done with **plastic plugs** inserted into drilled holes. Screws then expand the plug as they're driven. The manufacturer will state the correct size of masonry drill bit and choice of screw sizes for the plugs. The larger the screw, the stronger the fixing.

There are special plugs for light-weight cellular block (breeze block) walls.

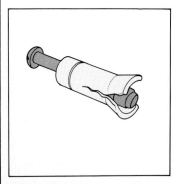

While plastic plugs and screws should be strong enough for almost any purpose you can also use **expansion bolts**, which are very strong. As they are available with hooks, they can be used for the type of shelves that hang on ropes or wires.

Cantilever brackets are high tensile steel rods that are set into holes in masonry walls. There is a plate in the middle to take a screw and plug, and then the rest of the rod goes into the hole in the back edge of the shelf. These brackets are invisible when the shelf is up.

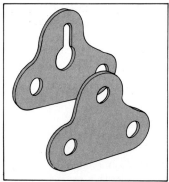

For fixing the tops of shelf units to walls, there are **mirror plates** and **cabinet hangers**, and **metal angle brackets** can be used to support the bottom of all but the heaviest ones.

Metal angle of various widths (usually aluminium) is sold in lengths and can be used instead of wood battens to support shelves. Thin ones look best with glass shelves.

Screw caps of plastic are made to fit cross-headed screws, and some also fit different sizes of countersunk holes. These are very useful for white melamine covered chipboard, as there is no way to refinish the holes made for fixings, and the rim around the edge of the caps hides any chipped edges around the hole.

Knock-down fittings are popular for fixing man-made boards together. To join two panels, simply screw one half of the fitting to each, and then bolt the two halves together. You need to design the shelves carefully to keep these fittings unobtrusive.

Screws should be woodscrews except, when fixing into chipboard, a different thread is needed.

Adjustable Shelf Supports

There are many ready-made lightweight shelf supports. Some are simply buttons with pins that are hammered into holes in the sides of the unit, while others have plastic studs that push into sockets inserted into the sides. You can also use short pieces of dowel (round hardwood) in snug fitting holes. There are metal supports for glass shelves.

A neat, invisible support is made of wire, the two ends fitting into holes in the side. A groove is made in the ends of the shelves from the back but not quite to the front. The shelves slide into the unit from the front, obscuring the wires.

All of these (apart from the wires) require one support at each corner of the shelf. You can put them in one place only, or drill four rows of holes in the sides to enable the supports and shelves to be raised or lowered.

Another way is to use bookcase strips. These are fixed to the sides and have metal clips that fit into slots. Four strips are needed.

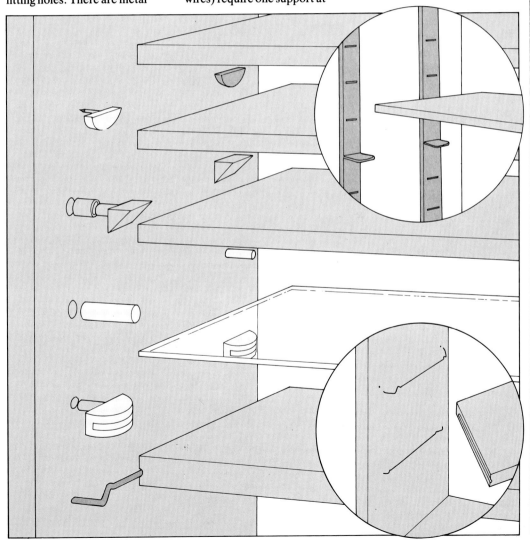

Tools and techniques

The first job you will come to is **cutting** the shelves to size. Any sharp hand-saw or power-saw will do. The important thing is to cut clean and straight. In the case of melamine and veneer, you must first score a line right through the decorative surface to prevent it breaking out. This is also the best way to cut wood cleanly.

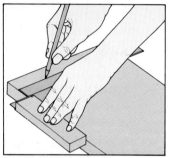

Use a setsquare or metal straightedge and a sharp knife to score a line all the way around the piece. But if only one side is to be seen, then you needn't worry about the other. Saw on the waste side, as near to the line as possible without chipping the edge you want to keep.

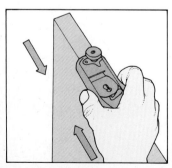

Plane the cut edge until it is flush with the scored line, always planing from the corner toward the middle. If you plane right across, the far edge will break out.

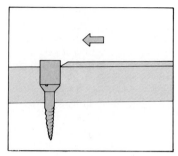

Boring neat holes can be a problem. Counterboring bits are available that cut holes exactly the size of screw heads. For wood, you can also get matched plug cutters that enable you to fill the hole with a plug of the same wood. Simply gluc in the plug (be sure the grain is in the same direction as the surrounding wood) and pare the surface flush with a chisel when set.

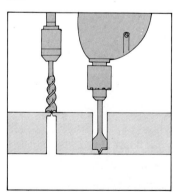

Large holes are best made with a brace and bit or a flat bit and power drill, working from each side toward the middle. As soon as the point comes through, turn the piece over.

Scribing is the technique of shaping panels so that they fit perfectly within the space, such as an alcove.

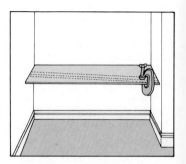

Cut a piece of thin scrap plywood or cardboard a little smaller than the space. You will need some ingenuity to find a way of holding it securely in place, with the front edge straight across the alcove. Battens slightly too long, wedged at the right height, are one way.

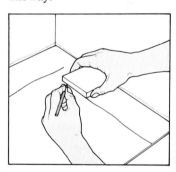

Using a pencil and small square piece of wood, trace a line around the three walls.

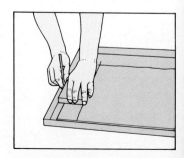

Then, place the template on the shelf material with the front edges flush, and transfer the lines onto the shelf. These are the lines to cut.

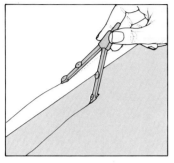

To scribe the back edge of a shelf to the wall, place it in position as near to the wall as possible, and set a pair of compasses to the width of the widest gap. Holding the compasses always at the same angle against the wall, mark the top of the shelf. Cutting this line will enable the shelf to touch the wall all along the edge.

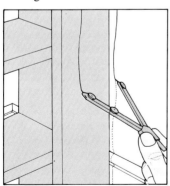

Use the same technique to scribe a wood trim for the side of a shelf unit. Temporarily fix the trim to the edge, keeping it straight with the upright, not the wall. Then set the compasses to the distance you want the trim to move toward the wall. Check that this is not smaller than the widest gap.

Edging with veneer or plastic is best done with the iron-on strip sold for the purpose.

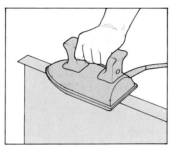

Simply cut off a piece a little too long and press it firmly over the edge with a medium hot iron. The adhesive melts quickly so there's no need to continue heating it for longer than 2 or 3 seconds. The important thing is to press it firmly. Allow it to cool.

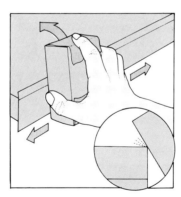

Then use a sanding block and medium to fine abrasive paper to weaken the edging, rubbing along the corner and bending it over. As you rub, gradually change the angle of the block until you're almost (but not quite) rubbing the face of the shelf. Repeat for the other edge.

Finally, use the sanding block or a fine file in this direction to trim the corners to a bevel.

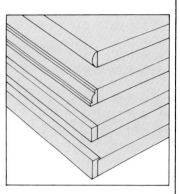

Using hardwood mouldings as **lippings** for blockboard, veneered chipboard or plywood makes a good-looking and more durable edge than iron-on strip. Mouldings are available in many shapes and some are made exactly the right width for man-made boards. Fix them with glue and small panel pins, setting the heads below the surface and filling with proprietary wood filler of an appropriate colour.

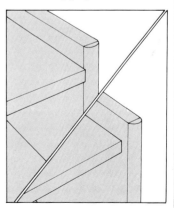

If you use shaped lippings, be careful when designing your shelves that the front edges don't meet like this, leaving a difficult mitre joint. It's easier to recess one panel behind the edge of the other.

TOP TEN TIPS

1. Consider getting all the pieces for your design cut to size by the supplier. Most of the hard work in making shelves is in the cutting, especially if you don't have room to support and manoeuvre large sheets.

2. If you plan to redecorate a hollow partition wall on which you will need fixings, find the studs beforehand and mark the positions on the skirting board.

Plan any redecoration to fit in with assembling built-in shelves. Painting or papering around shelves is messy and time-consuming.

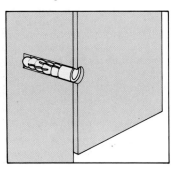

3. To make fixings to ceramic tiled walls, drill the holes very slowly with a masonry bit and make sure the plugs are inserted past the tile into the wall. That way, the expanding plug won't crack the tile when you tighten the screw.

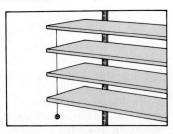

4. Line up the ends of shelves on track systems or brackets by fixing the top one first and then dropping a plumb line (or a weight on a string) down one side. Place each subsequent shelf just touching the string before fixing.

5. When putting shelf units next to a wall, make sure the front edge is carrying most of the weight. Fitted carpets usually rise next to the skirting board causing the unit to lean outward.

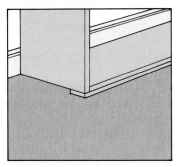

If the bottom is smooth, add a strip of wood to the underside at the front.

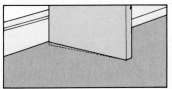

If it rests on uprights, you can cut away the back corners, or add adjustable feet to the front.

6. Self-adhesive rubber or foam pads will help keep glass shelves from slipping.

7. When fixing wood to the wall with plastic plugs, it's not necessary to drill all the holes in the wood first and them mark the wall. Drill through the wood and into the wall.

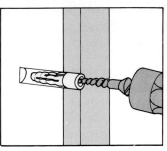

Insert a plug and tap it in flush. Then, insert a screw (without turning it) into the end of the plug and tap them into the hole. When the plug is at the correct depth, tighten up the screw. If you plan to fill the holes in the wood with wooden plugs, you can countersink the holes, and then drill through with the masonry bit.

This technique prevents any problems with holes being out of line with each other, and also means that you can adjust battens etc. with one screw in place.

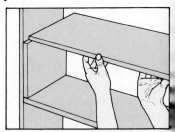

8. The easiest type of shelf unit to assemble has partitions

between the shelves. You can use the partitions to set the height of the shelves and support them while you fix them to the sides.

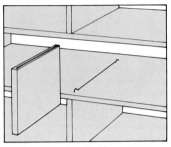

9. Invisible wire shelf supports are a good way to hold partitions

in place as well as shelves. This method also makes it easy to have the partitions in line with each other for a cube effect.

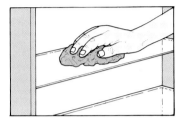

10. Glass shelves need frequent cleaning, so it's a good idea not to put them in hard to reach places.

Safety Tips

1. Make sure your shelves are strong enough for the load.

2. Don't leave a shelf unit temporarily leaning against a wall without making sure it won't fall or that children won't be able to climb on it.

3. Always get the advice of a glass supplier about the thickness and type of glass to use for shelves and have the edges ground and polished.

4. When using sharp-edged and power tools, always keep all parts of your body behind the cutting edge.

5. Make sure there are no electrical wires or pipes in an area of wall to be drilled.

6. Don't leave sharp-edged tools where there are children or pets.

7. Don't wear loose clothing or a tie when using power tools.

An interesting way of dividing open-plan living space is to construct a block-board partition with the required number of spaces and have the whole lot plastered. Additional shelves can be added afterwards and the plaster can be finished to fit in with the general decoration.

Author
Dek Messecar
Series Consultant Editor
Bob Tattersall
Design
Mike Rose and Bob Lamb
Picture Research
Liz Whiting
Editor
Alexa Stace
Illustrations
Rob Shone

Dek Messecar is a professional joiner who has had experience on all
aspects of DIY.

Bob Tattersall has been a DIY journalist for over 25 years and was
editor of Homemaker for 16 years. He now works as a freelance
journalist and broadcaster. Regular contact with the main DIY
manufacturers keeps him up to date on all new products and
developments. He has written many books on various aspects of DIY
and, while he is considered 'an expert', he prefers to think of himself as
a do-it-yourselfer who happens to be a journalist.

Photographs from Elizabeth Whiting
Photo Library by Clive Helm, Neil
Lorimer, Michael Nicholson, Julian
Neiman, Spike Powell and Jerry
Tubby.

Cover Photography by Clive Helm.
Equipment for cover photograph
supplied by Buck & Ryan Ltd.
London
Photograph page 7 courtesy of
Shelfstore Limited.

The Do It! Series was conceived, edited and designed by Elizabeth
Whiting & Associates and Rose & Lamb Design Partnership
for William Collins Sons & Co Ltd
© 1984 Elizabeth Whiting & Associates and Rose & Lamb Design
Partnership

First published 1984
Reprinted 1986, 1987
9 8 7 6 5 4 3 2 1
ISBN 0 00 411918 5

Published by William Collins Sons & Co Ltd
London · Glasgow · Sydney · Auckland
Toronto · Johannesburg

Printed in Spain